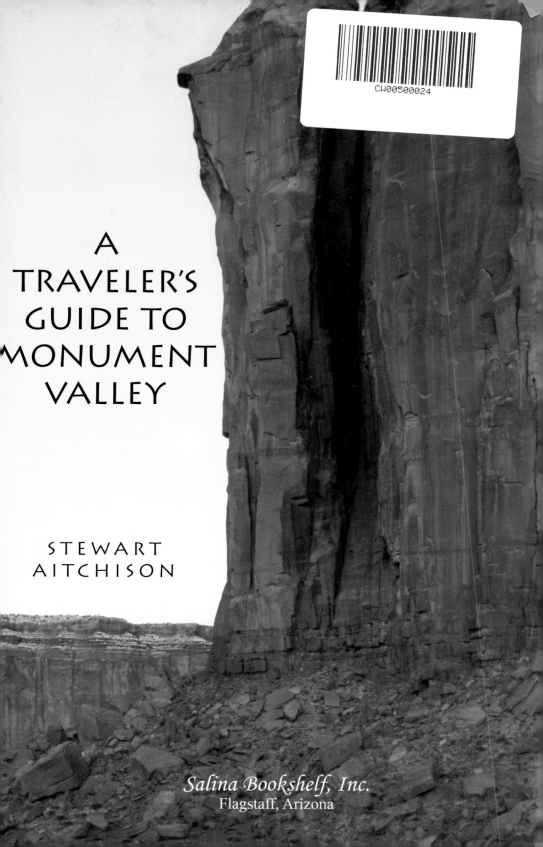

A TRAVELER'S GUIDE TO MONUMENT VALLEY

STEWART AITCHISON

Salina Bookshelf, Inc.
Flagstaff, Arizona

CONTENTS

Preceding page: The moon sets over Mitchell Mesa, named after one of the prospectors killed in Monument Valley in 1880. ▶

Right: Utah penstemon blooms from spring until early summer. The flower's deep carmine color and tubular shape are good clues that hummingbirds are its animal pollinators. ▶

INTO THE VALLEY

Through numerous western movies and, more recently, a multitude of commercials and advertisements, millions of people from around the world readily recognize the monoliths of Monument Valley. Despite the region's incredibly diverse topography, ranging from yawning chasms to saw-toothed, alpine mountains, it's Monument Valley's red sandstone buttes, mesas, and pinnacles that most people consider the quintessential image of the American Southwest.

Monument Valley is also an ancient home to the Native American. Is there anyone who cannot conjure up a mental picture, albeit stereotypical, of Navajo horsemen riding at a full gallop beneath the imposing Mittens or posing stoically on a rocky outcrop above the valley floor? Monument Valley Navajo Tribal Park, a nearly thirty thousand-acre parcel of land straddling the Utah-Arizona border in the heart of the Four Corners country, captures the imagination of those enamored with the mystique and legends of the Southwest. But is this the real Monument Valley? Let's take a trip into the valley for a closer look.

"Wóshdéé'" comes the welcome from the darkness of the interior of the hogan. I duck through the east-facing door into what seems at first a very dark room. But once inside, I see that the rustic juniper log interior is illuminated by a delicate golden sunbeam filtering down through the smoke hole.

Along the west wall is a space reserved for the camp matriarch. Susie Yazzie, of the Bitterwater Clan, sits with her legs folded beneath her (only men are supposed to sit cross-legged) on a sheepskin, vigorously carding wool. Her sheep are busy outside trying to find something to eat among the scrubby desert vegetation. Sand, twigs, and cockleburs drop out of the wool onto an apron cloth spread across Susie's lap. The wool she is working with is the select fleece from the back, shoulders, and flanks of the animal. The rest of the wool will be sold at the trading post.

With no particular urgency, for only the white man is always in a hurry, I stroll over to Susie. We exchange a softly spoken "ya'at'ééh" and an equally gentle handshake. Our eyes are diverted, for in traditional Navajo culture only rude people stare at each other.

Susie resumes her work. She takes the resulting fluffy roll of wool and deftly folds a bit of it into the strand of yarn wound on her spindle. Using her right hand, she rolls the spindle against her right thigh. With her left hand, she gently feeds out more and more wool. At intervals, she grasps the forming yarn with both hands and pulls on it. Not too hard, for that would break the yarn; yet not too gently, for that would leave the strand uneven and lumpy. From one small palm-size bundle of wispy fleece, Susie

Some Navajos consider the Big Indian to be a clown dancer with a coyote skin who circles the other participants in the Yei bei chei ceremony. ▶

According to the Navajos, the formation that the Anglos call King on His Throne actually comprises two dance leaders. The monoliths to the right and the left are Yei bei cheis, dancers impersonating the Holy People. ▶

Globemallow blooms from early spring into late summer. Navajos used these lovely wildflowers to make medicine for treating sore eyes and digestive disorders. ▶

spins several yards of tight, even yarn.

At her feet is an old, weathered ceremonial basket woven from strips of squawbush. The russet and black geometric designs have almost faded away, but their significance is still strong. The basket's center represents the beginning of life; coiling outward comes black rain clouds and the red of a clearing storm; the outer white coils represent the increasing population of the *Diné* (The People, as they traditionally call themselves); and the pathway of white cutting through the design to the end of the outer coil is to let The People emerge from a previous world into this one.

In the basket are leaves, roots, twigs, and short strands of yarn to show visitors the different colors obtained from plants used for dyeing. The orange root of the western dock produces yellow-brown, snakeweed or broomweed flowers and stems make yellow-green, and mountain mahogany yields russet. Gifts from the earth are used for other purposes as well: a section of yucca root makes soap to wash the yarn; a lump of chalky gypsum, in the mineral form of selenite, can be pulverized and sprinkled onto the fleece to absorb oil and dirt carried by the wool.

Susie moves to her upright loom. Traditionally, the loom would have been constructed out of rough pinyon pine, but hers is made of store-bought lumber. Susie makes herself comfortable on a low stool fashioned out of a milk crate covered with a sheepskin. With the pattern only in her mind, her well-practiced fingers take short lengths of weft yarn and carefully weave them into the warp threads.

Some rug buyers associate the Teec Nos Pos-style of tapestry weavings with Monument Valley. But Susie is weaving one of her favorite motifs, a Yei-style rug, in a design derived from ceremonial sand paintings and representing Navajo holy people. Rug styles that were once closely associated with a particular trading post or region of the Navajo country have spread throughout the reservation as Navajos and their ideas have become more mobile.

Anthropologists would have me believe weaving was introduced through Spanish and Pueblo Indian influence. But Navajo tradition relates:

Spider Woman instructed the Navajo women how to weave on a loom. The crosspoles were made of sky and earth cords, the warp sticks of sun rays, and the heddles of rock crystal and sheet lightning. The batten was a sun halo, and white shell made the comb. There were four spindles: one a stick of zigzag lightning with a whorl of cannel coal; one a stick of flash lightning with a whorl of turquoise; a third had a stick of sheet lightning with a whorl of abalone; a rain streamer formed the stick of the fourth and its whorl was white shell.

More guests have arrived, and custom dictates that food should be prepared for a feast. A juniper fire is started in the stove outside at the edge of the summer shade-house, a covered but open-sided structure that serves as a workspace and bedroom during hot weather and as an informal dining room.

A blackened coffee pot sits on the edge of the grill and mutton ribs roast. In a skillet, hot grease begins to smoke, while Susie and her daughter, Effie, are busy patting out round, flat pieces of soft flour dough. Each white tortilla-shaped piece of dough is cautiously lowered into the hot lard. Within seconds, the fry bread, *dah diniilghaazh*, puffs up and is ready to be turned over to brown the other side.

Lingering over another cup of strong coffee and munching on a piece of fry bread lathered with honey, we watch the sun dip below the ramparts of Mitchell Mesa. The upper cliffs of the west-facing buttes and mesas are ignited into crimson colors as the day fades into evening. Twilight seems endless; time stands still.

I let my mind drift. I wonder what it must have been like to be the first Navajos to enter the valley. Probably only a few extended families stayed. Water was always in short supply, and wild game, such as bighorn sheep and deer, were scarce. Over time the people acquired sheep, goats, and horses, but limited forage precluded any large herds. Hogans were traditionally built with east-facing doorways; summer shades were placed nearby. A few sandy swales were farmed by relying on runoff from the infrequent rains to water the crops of corn, beans, and squash.

Like the monuments themselves, the life of the people changed very little. But with the end of the nineteenth century came trading posts, missionaries, boarding schools, and all sorts of new and strange ideas. The changes in the Navajos' clothing, houses, and language were dramatic and are continuing today. Those of the older generation wear traditional dress, tie their long hair into a bun, may speak only Navajo, and live in hogans without running water or electricity. By contrast, their grandchildren wear the latest styles, cut their hair short, may speak only English, drive cars, and dream of college. Change is inevitable, but the tribal elders hope the children will remember and preserve their heritage.

Monument Valley's stark but awesome, sweeping beauty would be reason enough to visit the area. But the fact that the Navajo people, the *Diné*, live here blesses the region with a marvelous human dimension. The imposing silent monuments, mesas, and buttes are given a voice by the *Diné*. Come and experience this place The People call the "land of room enough and time enough."

In this old ceremonial basket are various roots, twigs, flowers, and minerals that help clean and dye the wool from the Navajos' sheep. ▶

Susie Yazzie, a resident of Monument Valley, demonstrates her fine skills as a weaver. Her favorite motif is the Yei-style, which depicts religious figures. ▶

9

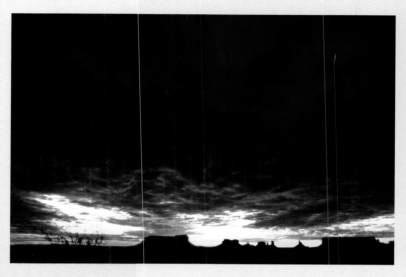

The view at sunrise from Harry Goulding's homestead (now Goulding's Lodge) in Monument Valley hasn't changed much since he and his wife Mike settled here in 1925. ▶

The Mittens are probably the most recognizable of all the Monument Valley buttes and mesas. They made their motion picture debut in the 1939 western classic Stagecoach *and have been a favorite backdrop ever since for movies and commercials.* ▶

The Anasazi carved numerous enigmatic figures, known as petroglyphs, into the dark desert varnish that coats some rocks and cliffs in Monument Valley. The varnish is a thin (less than a millimeter) layer of clay minerals containing oxides of manganese and iron, and trace amounts of more than thirty minor compounds, such as copper and zinc oxides. Amazingly, the varnish is produced by specialized bacteria (mixotrophs) that derive some of their energy from inorganic manganese. After a rain, the wet rock surface stimulates the proliferation of bacteria, which then secrete an enzyme that helps oxidize manganese and iron from dust that has blown across the rocks. ▶

THE ANCIENT ONES

"In the picturesque Monument Valley, where the dwindling remnants of great red buttes stand up in a fantastic array of pinnacles and towers. . . I have found no ruins in all this country, nor have I been able to learn of any from reliable Indians long resident upon the borders of this district."
T. Mitchell Prudden, 1903

The recent thundershower had scoured the dunes near the pothole arch called the Big Hogan. A few small chert pebbles sat perched on top of tiny pedestals of soft sand; pedestals protected from the corrosive action of rain by their capstones. Then I saw it. Not a rounded piece of quartz chert washed down from the mesa top like the others, but a triangular, chestnut-colored flake that an archaeologist would label a projectile point, but a layman like myself would call an arrowhead — not shaped by the forces of nature but crafted by human hands.

The stone point was perfect. Made in a style recognizable as prehistoric Anasazi, it was probably used by an ancient hunter after small game such as rabbits and squirrels or possibly larger quarry like deer or bighorn sheep. A thousand years later, Navajos occasionally collect such stone points to tip their own arrows or to prevent lightning from striking their hogan or to ward off other types of misfortune.

At the turn of the nineteenth century, no prehistoric human remains or artifacts in Monument Valley were recorded by T. Mitchell Prudden. Prudden was a Yale University professor of pathology with a passion for archaeology. Often alone, he spent several summers out West attempting to survey the entire San Juan River drainage (of which Monument Valley is a part) for archaeological remains. Perhaps Prudden can be forgiven for his cursory investigation, considering the difficulty of travel in his day over a roadless area larger than the state of West Virginia.

Seventy years later, a Museum of Northern Arizona survey revealed about fifty sites (a site being any evidence of human activity ranging from houses to petroglyph panels to lithic scatters, where rock tools were manufactured) just within the Tsé Biyi' Canyon portion of Monument Valley. Although all of the discovered sites are of Anasazi origin, archaeologists are virtually certain that, thousands of years prior to these people, nomadic hunters and gatherers also spent time here.

One day near the end of the Pleistocene, or great Ice Age, some eleven thousand or twelve thousand years ago, humans entered the Monument Valley area for the first time. These people, referred to as Paleo-Indians, were stalking big game — really big game, animals like wooly mammoths. The men were armed with spear-throwing atlatls. The spears were tipped with a distinctive form of stone point called Clovis, a fluted, lanceolate point averaging three to six inches in length. Just across the San Juan River to the north, on Lime Ridge, a possible encampment site containing a

There are many signs of the prehistoric Anasazi culture in Mystery Valley, a portion of Monument Valley Tribal Park that must be visited with a guide. ▶

To reach rainwater-filled potholes, the Anasazi carved precarious hand-and toe-holds into the soft sandstone. ▶

number of Clovis-style projectile points and stone flakes was discovered in 1985. A single point found in Little Capitan Valley, not far south of Monument Valley, may also have been left by these early hunters.

A thousand or so years later, the mammoth was extinct in the Southwest, and giant bison became the main prey item. They were killed with spears bearing a different style of stone point known as Folsom, also lanceolate but with delicate, pressure-flaked edges. Over the next couple of millennia, a series of characteristic unfluted stone points followed one another in popularity and are collectively called the Plano Complex. Little is known about any of these first inhabitants of Monument Valley, since their stone spearheads and tools are about the only artifacts that have survived the ages.

Over the next several thousand years, a continuing warming and drying climatic trend led to dramatic changes in plant and animal communities in the Southwest. Many of the large ice age mammals went extinct. Remaining herds of big game drifted eastward onto the Great Plains, followed by the Paleo-Indians. However, in the Southwest, a different group of people moved in. These people had a more generalized stone tool kit but still hunted wild game and gathered wild plant foods. This society, known as the Archaic Culture, evidently evolved first in the Great Basin (roughly the Nevada area) and Far West and then migrated into the Four Corners region (where the borders of Utah, Arizona, Colorado, and New Mexico meet).

▶ CLOVIS POINT

FOLSOM POINT

Unlike their predecessors, the Archaic people depended more and more on wild plant foods. Grinding stones, a basic component of their kitchen, were used to pulverize grasses and other seed crops into flour. Baskets, cordage, and nets of hair and vegetable fiber were carefully and skillfully made. And since the people frequently migrated from place to place in their never-ending search for food, only insubstantial brush huts were built for shelter.

By A.D. 200, several varieties of corn, which had been introduced through trade with people from Mexico, were becoming an important part of the Southwest diet. As novice farmers, some of the Archaic people slowly shifted away from a nomadic way of life to a more settled style. Instead of moving seasonally in concert with ripening wild foods, they placed more concentrated effort on tending planted crops. Crop surpluses were stored in circular cists, small pits lined with stone slabs. (Occasionally, the farmers used these same types of cists as crypts for their dead relatives.) They wove beautiful, watertight baskets and intricate yucca sandals. This emerging culture has been labeled Anasazi, a Navajo word often translated as the "ancient ones" but more

15

Most Anasazi houses were built using wattle-and-daub or stone blocks, but the small ruin in Echo Cave is constructed of loaves of clay. It's an unusual technique archaeologists call turtleback masonry. ▶

Vertical fractures called joints are readily visible in the upper DeChelly Sandstone part of the Big Indian. These cracks help maintain the sheerness of the upper sections of the monuments as the softer underlying claystone erodes and undermines the sandstone. ▶

16

closely meaning "enemy ancestors." This is a reference to the similarities between the ruins and relics of these prehistoric people and the houses and material goods of the contemporary Pueblo people who have occasionally been at odds with the Navajos.

Over several centuries, housing developed from brush shelters into well-made pithouses, one-room structures of log, brush, and mud, built partly underground for better insulation from the elements. Around A.D. 700, three significant events took place in the Anasazi world: the atlatl was replaced by the more accurate and versatile bow and arrow; the bean in three varieties (pinto, lima, and tepary) was added to their staple crop of corn, giving their diet a complete mix of proteins; and the people began to make pottery, providing a better way to cook. These innovations apparently allowed the Anasazi population to greatly increase around the Four Corners region. In some areas, families built apartment-like complexes, and a few constructed stone houses, the so-called cliff dwellings, in south-facing caves. Tens of thousands of people inhabited the region by the twelfth century.

However, unlike other locations in the Four Corners area, Monument Valley was probably never a big residential center. A general lack of water and abundance of clay soils limited farming opportunities and were not conducive to population growth. Some people lived in pithouses; a few built small stone masonry rooms against cliffs; and some lived high in cliff alcoves. A commonly visited ruin in Echo Cave is constructed of loaves of clay, an unusual technique called turtleback masonry. But other than the few ruins, about all that remains of the Anasazi's occupation of Monument Valley are petroglyphs incised into the dark desert varnish, painted pictographs, and a scattering of pottery shards. By the end of the 1300s, the Anasazi had abandoned Monument Valley, possibly moving southwesterly toward the Hopi Mesas, southeasterly toward the Rio Grande country, or both.

Shoshonean ancestors of the modern Utes and Southern Paiutes spread out of the Great Basin within the last thousand years and arrived in the Monument Valley area sometime after A.D. 1200 or 1300. Anthropologists also consider the Navajos as recent arrivals, probably first coming into the Four Corners region about 1500. While some anthropologists believe that the first Navajos didn't enter Monument Valley until the mid-1800s, at least some of today's Monument Valley residents claim a more ancient tie to the area.

Navajo tradition relates how The People emerged into this world from the Underworld between the Four Sacred Mountains — the San Francisco Peaks in Arizona, Mount Taylor in New Mexico, and Hesperus and Blanco Peaks in Colorado. The *Diné* wandered in the four cardinal directions to observe and learn about the surrounding world, which they found in terrible disarray and inhabited with horrible beasts. Eventually the Earth-Surface World was changed from monster-filled chaos into the well-ordered world of today's *Diné*.

Above: For at least four million sunrises, people have lived and died in the shadows of the great monuments. ▶

Right: Rain is scarce in Monument Valley, but during the summer it may come in a violent thunderstorm, what the Navajos call a male rain. With virtually no soil to absorb the downpour, the water runs off the rocky land and races toward the San Juan River. ▶

Inset: The Anasazi may have eaten the starchy underground bulb of the bent-stem mariposa lily. However, potential wild plant foods were probably always in meager supply in Monument Valley. The few pinyon pines would occasionally yield nuts; the seeds of the rice grass could be ground into a meal; yucca fruit was edible; and some of the annuals could be used as potherbs. The Anasazi's main diet consisted of the harvest from their small plots of corn, beans, and squash supplemented with wild game such as rabbits and deer. ▶

18

IT IS WRITTEN

". . . and scattered over the interval are many castle-like buttes and slender towers
. . . their forms wonderful imitations of the structures of human art. Illuminated
by the setting sun, the outlines of these singular objects came out sharp and distinct
. . . we could hardly resist the conviction that we beheld the walls and towers of some
Cyclopean city hitherto undiscovered in this far-off region."
J. S. Newberry, 1859

If seventeenth- or eighteenth-century Spanish explorers passed within sight of Monument Valley, they left no known written record. Mexicans raided as far north as Monument Valley for Indian slaves during the early 1800s, but apparently didn't bother to document the country they were passing through.

Possibly the first recorded description comes from Professor J. S. Newberry, a geologist attached to the J. N. Macomb Expedition which was looking for a supply route between the Rio Grande Valley and the settlements of southern Utah. In late August 1859, from a high point on the southeast flank of the Abajo Mountains, Newberry's pen gushed purple prose that may be a description of Monument Valley.

While Monument Valley's history prior to the 1850s is still largely a matter of conjecture, we do know that the outside world was crowding in on the Navajo. With the signing of the Treaty of Guadalupe Hidalgo in 1848, the rights of sovereignty of the Southwest, including the Four Corners area, passed from Mexico to the United States. To the Navajos, Utes, and Paiutes, this historic event held little immediate impact, but over the course of the following decades the natives' lives would be irrevocably changed.

Tragically, the majority of government officials that the Navajos came into contact with were neither understanding nor sympathetic to their needs or their predicament. Historians now feel that the Spaniards, and not the Navajos, were responsible for the warfare that erupted after the arrival of the Spanish. This legacy of the white man continued after the United States took control over the Southwest. The Navajos earned their reputation as warriors by fighting to protect their lands, property, and families as the white culture pursued Manifest Destiny. The traditional rights of Native Americans are still not respected.

Although a series of treaties between the Navajos and United States were drawn up, agreed to, and signed during the mid-1800s in an attempt to alleviate the conflicts, both sides continually failed to honor the terms. Finally in 1863, Brigadier General James H. Carleton set a course of all-out war against The People to "subdue them for all time or to annihilate them."

Harry and Mike Goulding built a two-story trading post at the base of Big Rock Door Mesa in the late 1920s. Eventually, Goulding's became the headquarters for filmmakers and tourists in Monument Valley. ▶

A Navajo father and daughter pause on Ford Point, named after film director John Ford, who made westerns in Monument Valley for over three decades. ▶

Sandhill muhly grass is gathered and tied together to make a Navajo hairbrush or bé' ézhóó'. ▶

To take care of the "Navajo problem," Colonel Christopher "Kit" Carson and the United States Army were ordered to round up the Indians and march them to an internment camp at Bosque Redondo near Fort Sumner, New Mexico. Using a scorched earth policy of killing livestock, devastating cornfields and orchards, and burning hogans, Carson and his troops were able to force the surrender of about eight thousand Navajos. Many died from starvation, disease, or exposure during the over three-hundred-mile "Long Walk" to Bosque Redondo in 1864.

One Navajo group that was able to escape Carson's men was led by Hoskininni ("Angry Warrior"). He and about sixteen family members fled from Monument Valley toward Navajo Mountain and then crossed the San Juan River into extremely rugged canyon country. While in pursuit, Carson noted the imposing dark monolith that the Navajos call 'Aghaałą́ and named it El Capitan because of its commanding position at the southern entrance to Monument Valley.

According to local resident Effie Yazzie Holiday, some of her ancestors were able to escape Carson and earlier, the Spanish, by fleeing to the top of Mitchell Mesa (also called Three Sisters Mesa).

After four heart-breaking years, the Navajos at Bosque Redondo negotiated a treaty with the U.S. government and were allowed to return to their homeland. Shortly after this treaty was signed, Hoskininni and his people came out of hiding and returned to Monument Valley. The next dozen years were fairly peaceful, until a new type of invader entered the valley.

It was New Year's Eve, 1880. James Merrick (sometimes recorded as Merritt) and Ernest Mitchell encountered a party of four Mormon scouts who were returning from Montezuma Creek to the Colorado River. At the river, a wagon train was camped and awaiting word on whether or not a passable route across southeast Utah had been found. The two prospectors and the four scouts traveled together west across Comb Ridge down into Comb Wash, where Merrick and Mitchell forded the San Juan River and headed south toward Monument Valley. Merrick had told George Hobbs, one of the scouts, that he knew where the Navajos had a smelter and were handling ore that assayed 90 percent silver. He and Mitchell were going to look for the Indian mine.

Since returning to their homeland in 1868, the Navajos' production of silver buckles, buttons, clasps, and other items had led to rumors of secret silver mines. After several weeks passed and the two prospectors did not return, an armed search party went out in February to look for them. The party located the bodies of Merrick and Mitchell, scalped and covered with rocks and brush, near the buttes that now bear their names. Local Navajos said that Paiutes had committed the murders, but Paiutes pleaded innocence. According to a search party sent out to locate the two men, specimens of "very rich quartz ores" were found near the bodies. "Obviously," the men had discovered the mine and had been killed on their way out.

The ubiquitous turquoise and silver jewelry worn by Navajos led many early prospectors to believe that a secret silver mine existed somewhere in the Navajo country. Although the occurrence of a silver mine in the Monument Valley area has been discounted by most geologists, it is worth noting that the only known commercial body of silver ore in sandstone in the United States was discovered in the Silver Reef Sandstone, a member of the Chinle Formation. The Chinle Formation occurs in Monument Valley but apparently the Silver Reef Member does not. Or does it? ▶

All the components of a good lost mine legend were present: hazy rumors that early Spanish explorers had known of the silver mine; the alleged discovery of the mine and subsequent killing of Merrick and Mitchell; and rugged, wild country guarded by Indians. So, despite the dangers, others followed in Merrick and Mitchell's footsteps.

In March 1884, after outfitting at H.L. Mitchell's (father of the slain Ernest) Trading Post (near present-day Aneth), two Easterners, Samuel Walcott and James McNally, ventured into Monument Valley. They, too, were killed. Tension between the whites and Navajos nearly erupted in war, but was quelled when Hoskininni, as the head of the Monument Valley Navajos, was arrested for the murders. He spent two months in jail before being released since no evidence for his involvement came to light. Historians speculate that his son Hoskininni-begay, who was never charged, probably committed the crime.

Fry bread has become a Navajo staple in the last century. Before they were rounded up by U.S. troops in 1863, the Navajos were not familiar with flour derived from wheat, only corn flour. While held captive at Bosque Redondo in New Mexico, the Navajo women learned from the local Hispanics how to make sopapillas or fry bread, using wheat flour. A typical recipe consists of making a soft dough from 3 cups white flour, 1 1/4 teaspoons baking powder, 1/2 teaspoon salt, and about 1 1/3 cups warm water. Take about a golf ball-sized piece of dough and pat out into a quarter-inch thick pancake. Drop into about a half-inch of hot shortening in a cast iron frying pan, preferably outside over a juniper fire. Cook to a golden brown. Turn once. ▶

To prevent further white encroachment and further bloodshed, President Chester A. Arthur legitimized the Navajo claim to the region south of the San Juan River to Monument Valley by Executive Order in 1884. Later, realizing that part of the land was claimed by Paiutes, President Benjamin Harrison rescinded Arthur's Executive Order in 1892 and created what became known as the "Paiute Strip." Then in 1923, the Paiutes moved to a more fertile section of land in southeast Utah and the strip was opened to homesteading. The strip was returned to the Navajos (minus several homesteads including Goulding's) by legislative act on March 1, 1933.

The first Anglos to come to the Monument Valley area with the idea of starting a business rather than searching for lost mines were John and Louisa Wetherill. This young couple from Mancos, Colorado, was warned that the Indians would kill them. Undaunted, they came to Oljato "Moonlight Water" to start a trading post in the spring of 1906. Hoskininni-begay asked them to leave but John suggested

a rabbit hunt and feast. Finally Hoskininni-begay and his father agreed that the Wetherills could stay. The Wetherills later started a second post that eventually grew into the community of Kayenta.

The early part of the twentieth century saw the arrival of the first tourists in Monument Valley. One of these was Western writer Zane Grey who visited the area with John Wetherill in 1913. Grey recounts in his autobiographical *Tales of Lonely Trails*:

> My first sight of Monument Valley came with a dazzling flash of lightning. It revealed a vast valley, a strange world of colossal shafts and buttes of rock, magnificently sculptured, standing isolated and aloof, dark, weird, and

A traditional Navajo camp consists of a hogan with an east-facing door (a snug refuge during inclement weather), and a summer shade that is constructed so that breezes can filter through it. To the right of the shade is a smaller hoganlike structure that serves as a sweat lodge. ▶

lonely. When the sheet lightning flared across the sky showing the monuments silhouetted black against that strange horizon, the effect was marvelously beautiful. I watched until the storm died away....Dawn, with the desert sunrise, changed Monument Valley, bereft it of its night glow and weird shadow and showed it in another aspect of beauty....I rode down the sweet-scented sage slopes under the shadow of the lofty Mittens and around and across the valley. And when I had completed my ride a story had woven itself into my mind; and the spot where I stood was to be the place where Lin Stone taught Lucy Bostil to ride the great stallion Wildfire.

The main ancestral line of sheep introduced by the early Spaniards was the churro, a variety noted for its long, straight wool, which is well suited for hand spinning. Today, however, the most common Navajo sheep tends to be a mixture of strains of Spanish Merino and French Rambouillet that were brought in the late 1800s. The modern sheep yield better mutton but shorter, kinkier wool. The churro sheep were practically extinct until Utah State University, under the direction of Dr. Lyle McNeal, began an effort in the 1970s to propagate this breed in order to increase the value of textiles woven by Navajos and Hispanics. Churros are slowly being reintroduced on the reservation. ▶

Another early tourist was a self-proclaimed "tenderfoot and cliff-dweller from Manhattan." Charles Bernheimer engaged the guiding services of John Wetherill for the summers of 1919 through 1924. Although a businessman by trade, Bernheimer had a keen interest in exploring the slickrock canyons of the Southwest looking for Indian ruins. On a 1921 expedition under the auspices of the American Museum of Natural History, Bernheimer wrote in his diary:

> Looking east from Navajo Mountain the sunset was a marvel of color. Monument Valley lay before us, three thousand feet below. Each visible monument, and there seemed to be no end of them, glowed in an orange-red fire, each bordered on its easterly face by a strongly contrasting blue-slate shadow. The monuments looked like shooting jets of fire, their purple-grey shadows like smoke.

On a hot autumn day in 1921, a young sheepherder from Colorado, Harry Goulding, crested Comb Ridge and caught sight of Monument Valley for the first

By mid-Permian time, a vast desert was forming across northeastern Arizona. Hot, dry winds piled quartz sand into mountainous dunes hundreds of feet high, patterned with ripples. As more and more sediment was added to the deposit, the buried sand was slowly cemented together with silica and calcium carbonate "glue" into the three hundred- to six hundred-feet-thick sandstone called DeChelly. Today, groundwater seeping through the stone can dissolve some of the cement and grains of sand fall off leaving small depressions in the cliff face. Given enough time, this process continues until a large cave forms. ▶

sandstone along with the softer claystone form the slopes that encircle the base of the monument. Through time the larger mesas are reduced in size to buttes, all the while continuing to display the classic profile of a monument.

All the stages of monument development are wonderfully displayed in the valley, which of course is not a valley at all in the usual sense. And what will become of today's monuments? They, too, will succumb to the forces of time and erosion, but Gene Foushee tells us not to worry: Future monument valleys will no doubt form where a massive sandstone overlies a massive claystone. "The extraordinary monuments are simply the children of the mesas."

The origin of the landscape has been told, but what about the origin of the rock layers themselves? The oldest rock exposed in Monument Valley is Cedar Mesa Sandstone, which was laid down as sand in a shallow marine environment in early Permian time (the Permian Period lasted from 286 to 245 million years ago). The tourist road crosses the top of the Cedar Mesa Sandstone in a wash just after descending from the visitor center.

As time passed, the area became more of a wet tidal flat with streams and rivers flowing westerly and southwesterly from a massive mountain range, the Uncompahgre Range, several hundred miles to the northeast. The rivers carried heavy sediment loads of granitic and gneissic material and deposited them on the coastal lowlands. The boulders and larger pebbles settled out first, close to the mountains; the finer sand, clay, and silt were carried farther by the sluggish rivers and deposited as red beds six hundred to seven hundred feet thick, from the vicinity of Canyonlands National Park south through Monument Valley and west toward the Grand Canyon region.

At this time primitive amphibians and reptiles roamed the lowlands, and plant fossils indicate that the environment was arid. Geologists have named these red deposits the Organ Rock after an erosional feature that resembles a pipe organ west of Monument Valley.

By mid-Permian time, the sea attempted to encroach from the west but reached only a little east of where the Grand Canyon would one day form. From the shoreline eastward, a vast desert formed as hot, dry winds piled quartz sand into mountainous dunes hundreds of feet high, patterned with ripples. The individual fine sand grains are often coated with iron oxide, giving a reddish-orange cast to them. As more and more sediment was added to the deposit, the buried sand was slowly cemented together with silica and calcium carbonate "glue" into a three-hundred- to six-hundred-feet-thick sandstone called DeChelly.

Until the end of the Permian, the Monument Valley area remained a desert coastal lowland that was either gently eroding or with little or no additional sedimentation taking place. The Uncompahgre Mountains were nearly leveled, and the few meandering streams were virtually clear of sediment.

Through Triassic, Jurassic, and Cretaceous time (about 245 to 65 million years ago), as the region fluctuated between coastal mud flats, swamps, and deserts, other deposits of sedimentary rocks were added to the geologic layer cake. However, in Monument Valley, most of these thousands of feet of younger layers of rock have been stripped away over the last 65 million years as the Colorado Plateau (the geologist's designation for the Four Corners region) has been uplifted a mile or more above sea level. A few of the mesas and monuments are still capped with remnants of the Moenkopi Formation and Shinurump Member of the Chinle Formation.

Left top: Unlike the majority of the monuments, which are erosional remnants of layers of sedimentary rock, 'Aghaałą is a volcanic neck, the solidified magma that once filled a now-eroded vent leading up to a volcano. According to older Navajos, 'Aghaałą is one of several monoliths in the area that help hold up the sky. ▶
Left bottom: Virga showers, wisps of precipitation streaming from a cloud that evaporate before reaching the ground, are not uncommon during late summer. ▶

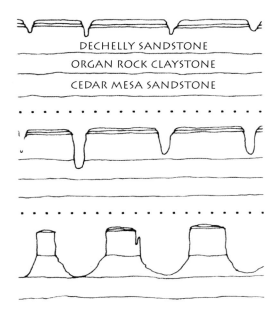

DECHELLY SANDSTONE
ORGAN ROCK CLAYSTONE
CEDAR MESA SANDSTONE

LANDSCAPE DEVELOPMENT

Look around Monument Valley, and you'll see examples of each stage of monument development: a plateau divided into smaller mesas, which in turn are eroded into buttes and spires. Over time, vertical cracks or joints in the DeChelly Sandstone are widened by rain, creating individual mesas. Erosion of the softer Organ Rock Claystone slopes around the base of the monuments undercuts the overlying sandstone. Then the unsupported sandstone cliff breaks along a joint resulting in the large mesas being reduced into smaller buttes. Most of the major formations in the valley today have been present since the beginning of the Pleistocene Ice Age, about two million years ago. As geologist Gene Foushee eloquently explains, "The extraordinary monuments are simply the children of the mesas." ▶

Rain slowly erodes the DeChelly Sandstone into individual grains of sand that are washed down drainages and then blown by the prevailing winds into dunes. ▶

Whether you approach the Monument Valley area from the south or north on U.S. Highway 163, some of the first "monuments" you see are not the typical erosional remnants of reddish sedimentary rock, but rather are solitary towers of black rock that, according to Navajo lore, help hold up the sky. Alhambra Rock to the north and 'Aghaałá to the south are geologically volcanic necks, the solidified material that once filled a now-eroded vent possibly leading to a volcano. Some of these igneous features seem to have been created by the explosive energy of gas-charged magmas drilling through enclosing sedimentary rock.

Probably by the time of the Pleistocene Ice Age, Monument Valley was looking very much like what we see today, at least in terms of major topographic features. However, a closer examination of the past environment would reveal fewer deep washes and decidedly different plants and animals than today. Where there are now stands of blackbrush, during the Pleistocene there were woodlands of pinyon pine and juniper. Where the pinyon-juniper woodlands now grow probably would have been Douglas fir forests. Ice Age temperatures were considerably cooler than today's climate, and there were more permanent streams and springs. Near the formation called the Totem Pole, what is now just sandy desert were small freshwater ponds teeming with minute snails and other freshwater invertebrates.

During the last two million years, the Monument Valley area was apparently subjected to alternating periods of sand and clay sedimentation and erosion. Evidence suggests that at the end of the Pleistocene, about ten thousand years ago, the climate was more humid and cooler than it is at present. This was a time of more deposition than erosion, of mammoth herds, and probably of the first human hunters.

The cyclic nature of climatic change continued. Dry desert winds blew sand into great dunes during an erosional phase. After a few thousand years, a moister and cooler climate returned. Streams flowed through the valley creating small lakes and depositing sediments. Artifacts of the early Anasazi date from this time (100 B.C. to A.D. 700). Then a drier climate and arroyo cutting returned, ending about the time the Anasazi left Monument Valley (A.D. 1250). (These harsher growing conditions probably stimulated the Anasazi's departure from the valley.) This was followed by yet another period when deposition gained over erosion, lasting from A.D. 1300 to 1700 and accompanied by warm and dry weather.

By the 1880s, the continued drying of the climate and increasing numbers of livestock initiated the present state of erosion. Nearly all the deep arroyos and washes cut into the soft sandy sediments seen today around Monument Valley have formed in the last hundred years. Sand derived from eroding DeChelly cliffs is washed down arroyos, the water evaporates, and southwesterly winds pile the fine sand into huge dunes against the mesas.

Above: *The muddy San Juan River has incised a deep, intricate, meandering canyon north of the Monument Valley.* ▶

Right: *Blocks of DeChelly Sandstone may spall off as the softer underlying Organ Rock Claystone erodes away, undercutting the massive sandstone wall. The DeChelly cleaves along vertical cracks or planes of weakness, which are probably the result of stress as the region has been uplifted over the last sixty-five million years.* ▶

The Monument Valley landscape of today is thus an interplay of geologic and climatic forces with some finishing touches added by human activity. In 1937, two years before his death, Hoskininni-begay summarized his perception of the present human condition in Monument Valley:

> Most of our people are poor now, like I am. Many of them blame John Collier [Commissioner of Indian Affairs], who made us reduce our flocks and herds because there was not enough grass for all. But I think the true reason is a change in the climate. When I was a young man this whole country was covered with tall grass. We had rains enough in summer to keep it alive and growing. Now the rains do not come and the grass dies. There are fewer sheep and horses now than when my family claimed this valley, yet all you can see is sand. The grass is gone. All we need to be rich again is rain.

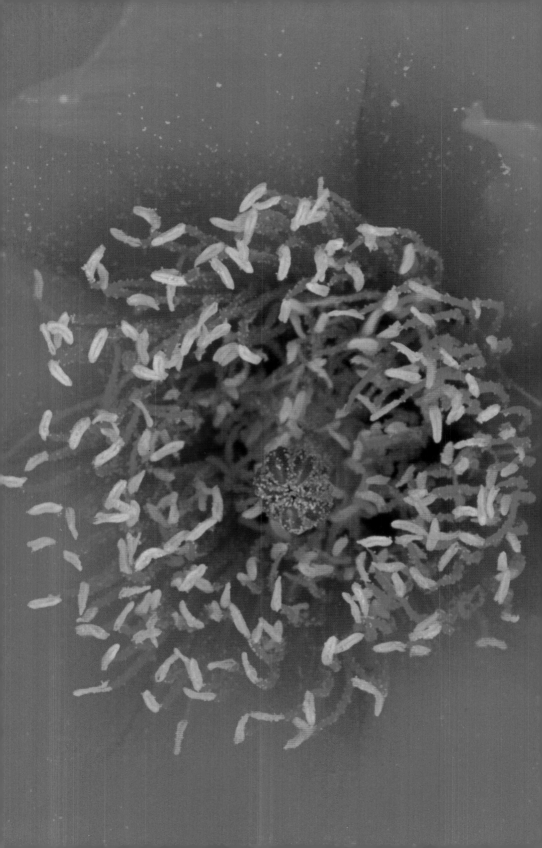

LIVING IN THE DESERT

"There is a treeless place amid the rocks."
Translation of an old Navajo name for Monument Valley

It is a bright, exceptionally clear autumn day. From the lookout at the visitor center my eyes are caught by the hulking masses of red stone that make up the Left and Right Mittens. The tiny gray-black dots of vegetation between the monuments are scarcely noticeable in this scene set on a grand scale. The towering rocks and endless, azure sky overwhelm the visitor.

My family and I begin to descend the tourist road to the floor of the valley and notice that there are bushes, flowers, and even a few small trees. There is life in this desert.

As we reach the valley floor, which consists primarily of an old Pleistocene-age surface of coalescing alluvial fans, we see predominantly blackbrush interspersed with a few other hardy shrubs and an occasional wildflower, the product of a recent rain shower. As we approach a turnout for another look at the Mittens, the road skirts a large sandy hill on the left. This past spring was a relatively wet one (perhaps an inch or two of moisture fell over a three-month period), and for a short time, the sand was covered with flowers and grasses — evening primrose, indigo-bush, dwarf lupine, crownbeard, cryptantha, prickly poppy, fleabane daisy, globemallow, phacelia, desert marigold, scarlet penstemon, western dock, desert peppergrass, sand verbena, Gray's biscuit root, sand gilia, milk vetch, Indian rice grass, and galleta grass. Many of these delicate spring-blooming plants are annuals, quickly producing seed and then disappearing until the next season. Now at the end of the summer "rainy season," mostly perennials are providing a showy display: rabbitbrush, broom snakeweed, and sulphurflower are ablaze with golden flowers. A few purple sage plants still fill the air with their strong, minty, volatile terpene oils. A new crop of tumbleweed, an introduced weed from the steppes of Russia, is drying out and turning brown, ready for winter winds to blow them hither and yon, spreading seeds.

The blackbrush, a member of the rose family, is well suited to living on the clay and stony flats, as evidenced by its extensive stands. Mormon tea, four-wing saltbush, and shadscale grow scattered among the blackbrush. After the road crosses Stagecoach Wash and threads its way along the base of Elephant Butte and Camel Butte, the deep red clay layers of the Organ Rock Claystone form an exceptionally hostile environment for plant growth. Amazingly, during most springs, a profusion of bent-stem (also called weakstem) mariposa lilies bloom here. These determined

Frigid winter temperatures limit the types of cactus that can live in Monument Valley. Prickly-pear cactus is found in protected, south-facing locations where freezing is uncommon. ▶

Above: *Unusually wet winters and springs can result in a brief but spectacular profusion of wildflowers.* ▶

Left top: *The legendary tumbleweed is actually a native of the steppes of Eurasia and supposedly immigrated to North America in the late 1800s in a shipment of Russian wheat. Tumbleweed, also known as Russian thistle, quickly invades land that has been overgrazed.* ▶

Left bottom: *On the dry, hostile, red clay slopes beneath the Three Sisters, delicate bent-stem mariposa lilies bloom after spring showers.* ▶

perennials are closely related to the sego lily, the state flower of Utah, whose starchy, underground bulb nourished the Mormon pioneers. On this lovely fall day, however, there is no evidence that any plant ever manages to grow at this spot.

Why this diversity of plant species on sand, as opposed to the rockier soils? The sand quickly absorbs any rain, but as that moisture percolates downward, it encounters the impervious claystone underneath. At this contact the water stops; the sand insulates the water from evaporating, and plants with long roots can tap this water source. Growing directly on the claystone or in the rocky soils is a much more difficult proposition.

The importance of water is again emphasized as we drive over a wash. Along the sides of the wash grow the shaggy-barked cliffrose, squawbush, desert ash, and wispy tamarisk, an exotic species that is native to Arabian and Mideastern deserts and came to the American Southwest via transplants to California. Against the base of a cliff, especially those walls facing north away from the sun, can be found netleaf hackberry, Utah serviceberry, and mountain privet, also known as desert olive. Here they benefit

Tamarisk is an exotic species, native to the Mediterranean, that has become widespread in the American Southwest. Typically, it takes root along washes and stream banks and successfully competes against native plants. ▶

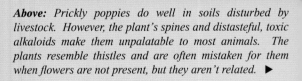

Above: *Prickly poppies do well in soils disturbed by livestock. However, the plant's spines and distasteful, toxic alkaloids make them unpalatable to most animals. The plants resemble thistles and are often mistaken for them when flowers are not present, but they aren't related.* ▶

Left: *Canaigre, also called western dock or wild rhubarb, has tuberous roots that contain tannin. Besides using the root as a dye source, Navajos apply a root-and-leaf concoction to sores.* ▶

The young, shreddy bark of the cliffrose was once used by Navajos in Monument Valley to line cradleboards. The shredded bark is more absorbent than cotton and can be reused after drying in the sun. ▶

Above: *Snakeweed, or broomweed, may cover more acres than any other perennial plant in Navajoland. It has many medicinal and ceremonial uses, including being very effective in treating insect stings. Simply chew a little piece and apply the pulp to the wound.* ▶

Right: *Ironically, the leaves of the squawbush are used to treat the effects of the closely related poison ivy. The red berries can be eaten raw or cooked. Navajo baskets are made from strips of squawbush wood.* ▶

from runoff down the rock surface.

One group of plants that is conspicuous by its absence is the cacti. If we search, we can find some prickly pear and hedgehog cactus, but winters are too severe for most species.

We head over to the Big Dune at the northeast base of Thunderbird Mesa. This year's unusually rainy May and June has allowed many plants to bloom on this normally barren dune. Acres of the dune are covered with a pale green bush one to two feet tall but unfamiliar to any of us (it is later identified as gray sand plant, a new species to us). Amazing what a little rain can do. Another strange plant poking here and there out of the sand like a foot-high, purplish yellow rod is the fleshy broomrape. This odd-looking plant lacks chlorophyll, which would allow it to photosynthesize its own food. Instead, it must be parasitic on other plants such as sagebrush, cactus, and wild buckwheat. But here, on the fairly barren dune, who is its host? Maybe a future botanist will unravel the mystery.

One of the great ways to explore a dune is to look at the patterns in the sand. Wind-created ripples are an obvious feature, but a closer look reveals the comings and goings of a variety of primarily nocturnal creatures. There are the tractor-like tracks of darkling or stink beetles and scorpions; the miniscule paw prints of pocket mice; the slightly larger prints of a hopping kangaroo rat; the s-curves of a snake, maybe one of the small races of prairie rattlesnake; and the thin toe prints and tail-drag of a lizard — perhaps a plateau whiptail, a strange beast in that it comes only in the female gender. Plateau whiptails reproduce by a process called parthenogenesis, where one female plays the role of a male, stimulating another female's body into producing hormones to cause her eggs to grow into genetic clones of herself.

Scattered across the dune are tiny quarter-inch-diameter holes, surrounded by a little fencelike structure of sticks and grains of sand all held together with a few strands of spider silk. These are the burrows of the wolf spider, a spider that doesn't waste its time building a web and hoping a bug flies into it but rather spends most of its days patiently sitting at the burrow's entrance waiting to grab a passing insect.

Churned-up piles of sand near the base of the dune probably mean a pocket gopher has been busy digging tunnels in search of plant roots to eat. A two-inch hole in the sand at the base of a rabbitbrush is the entrance to a white-tailed antelope squirrel's burrow. It's not long before we see one of these squirrels running across the dune with its tail held up over its back like a parasol. It is chipmunk in size and coloration and is one of the few mammals in the desert that can remain active during the heat of a summer day. The squirrel's body temperature can rise above 110 degrees Fahrenheit without ill effect. If it starts to get too hot, it salivates on its fur to promote evaporative cooling or scurries into its dark, cool burrow to unload heat.

50

PARK INFORMATION

Monument Valley Navajo Tribal Park
P.O. Box 360289
Monument Valley, UT 84536
435-727-3287 or 435-727-3353

Navajo Parks and Recreation Department
P.O. Box 9000
Window Rock, AZ 86515
928-871-6647

GUIDES & TOURS

Arizona Horseback Vacations
5580 South Kings Ranch Road
Gold Canyon, AZ 85218
480-982-7822

Bennett Tours
Monument Valley, UT 84536
435-727-3283

Bigman's Horseback Tours
Kayenta, AZ 86033
928-674-1522

Edward Black's Monument Valley Trail Rides
P.O. Box 310155
Mexican Hat, UT 84531
800-551-4039; 435-739-4285

Far Out Expeditions (naturalist-led)
P.O. Box 307
Bluff, UT 84512
435-672-2294
www.faroutexpeditions.com

Fred's Adventure Tours
P.O. Box 310308
Mexican Hat, UT 84531
435-739-4294

Goulding's Tours
P.O. Box 360001
Monument Valley, UT 84536
800-874-0902 or 435-727-3231
www.gouldings.com

Roland's Navajoland Tours
928-697-3524

Sacred Monument Tours
P.O. Box 362530
Monument Valley, UT 84536
435-727-3218
www.monumentvalley.net

Totem Pole Tours
435-727-3313
www.totempoletours.com

NEARBY ACCOMMODATIONS

Monument Valley

Goulding's Lodge and Campground
P.O. Box 360001
Monument Valley, UT 84536
800-874-0902 or 435-727-3231
or 435-727-3280
www.gouldings.com

Monument Valley Navajo Tribal Park
Campground
    P.O. Box 360289
    Monument Valley, UT 84536
    435-727-3287

Kayenta

Hampton Inn
    Hwy 160
    Kayenta, AZ 86033
    800-531-0202 or 928-697-3170

Holiday Inn
    P.O. Box 307
    Kayenta, AZ 86033
    800- HOLIDAY or 928-697-3221

Best Western Wetherill Inn
    P.O. Box 175
    Kayenta, AZ 86033
    800-WESTERN or 928-697-3231

Mexican Hat

Burch's Motel & RV Park
    P.O. Box 310337
    Mexican Hat, UT 84531
    435-683-2221

Canyonlands Motel
    P.O. Box 310187
    Mexican Hat, UT 84531
    435-683-2230

Mexican Hat Lodge
    P.O. Box 310175
    Mexican Hat, UT 84531
    435-683-2222

San Juan Inn & Trading Post
    P.O. Box 310276
    Mexican Hat, UT 84531
    800-447-2022 or 435-683-2220

Valley of the Gods B&B
    P.O. Box 310307
    Mexican Hat, UT 84531
    970-749-1164

Bluff

Calf Canyon B&B
    P.O. Box 218
    Bluff, UT 84512
    435-672-2470

Desert Rose Inn & Cabins
    P.O. Box 148
    Bluff, UT 84512
    888-475-ROSE or 435-672-2303

Kokopelli Inn
    P.O. Box 27
    Bluff, UT 84512
    435-672-2322 or 800-541-8854

Mokee Motel
    P.O. Box 324
    Bluff, UT 84512
    435-672-2242

Pioneer House B&B
    P.O. Box 219
    Bluff, UT 84512
    888-637-2582 or 435-672-2446

Recapture Lodge
    P.O. Box 309
    Bluff, UT 84512
    435-672-2281

GLOSSARY TO NAVAJO WORDS

Bilagáanas
white people

bé' ézhóó'
hairbrush

dah díníilghaazh
fry bread

Dibé Nineez
Navajo name for Harry Goulding;
literally, "sheep he is tall"

Diné
The (Navajo) People

T'iis Názbąs
A trading post in northeast Arizona;
literally, "place of cottonwoods"

Tsé Biyi'
Part of Monument Valley; literally,
"within the rock"

Tséch' ízhí
name of a Monument Valley mesa;
literally, "rough rock"

wóshdę́ę́'
welcome; literally, "from here to
there"

yá'át'ééh
hello; literally, I am well

yéi
a god

yéi bei chei
human dancer impersonating a god

INDEX

FURTHER READING

GENERAL

DeRoos, Robert William. 1965. *Monument Valley*. Flagstaff, AZ: Northland Press.

Klinck, Richard. 1958. *Land of Room Enough and Time Enough*. Albuquerque, NM: University of New Mexico Press.

McPherson, Robert S. 1992. *Sacred Land, Sacred View: Navajo Perceptions of the Four Corners Region*. Provo, UT: Charles Redd Center for Western Studies, Brigham Young University.

Miller, Joseph. 1951. *Monument Valley and the Navajo Country*. New York, NY: Hastings House Publishers.

Ortiz, Alfonso. 1983. *Handbook of North American Indians: Southwest, Volume 10*. Washington, D.C.: Smithsonian Institution, U.S. Government Printing Office.

PREHISTORY

Benally, Clyde with Andrew O. Wiget, John R. Alley, and Garry Blake. 1982. *Dineji Nakee' Naahane': A Utah Navajo History*. Monticello, UT: San Juan School District.

Correll, J. Lee. 1971. "Navajo Frontiers in Utah and Troublous Times in Monument Valley." *Utah Historical Quarterly* 39(2): 145-161.

Crotty, Helen K. 1983. *Honoring the Dead: Anasazi Ceramics from the Rainbow Bridge-Monument Valley Expeditions*. Los Angeles: Monograph Series, Museum of Cultural History, University of California, #22.

Davis, William E. 1989. "The Lime Ridge Clovis Site." *Utah Archaeology* 1989 2(1): 66-76.

Dorn, Ronald I. 1991. "Rock Varnish." *American Scientist* 79(6): 542-553.

Neely, James A. and Alan P. Olson. 1977. *Archaeological Reconnaissance of Monument Valley in Northeastern Arizona*. Anthropology Research Report #3, Museum of Northern Arizona, Flagstaff, AZ.

Nickens, Paul R. 1982. "A Summary of the Prehistory of Southeastern Utah" in *Contributions to the Prehistory of Southeastern Utah*, Cultural Resource Series No. 13, Bureau of Land Management, Salt Lake City, UT.

Prudden, T. Mitchell. 1903. "The Prehistoric Ruins of the San Juan Watershed of Utah, Arizona, Colorado and New Mexico". *American Anthropologist* 5(2): 224-288, Lancaster, PA.

HISTORY

Christenson, Andrew L. 1987. "The Last of the Great Expeditions: The Rainbow Bridge - Monument Valley Expeditions 1933-38." *Plateau* 58(4): 1-32.

Gillmor, Frances, and Louisa Wade Wetherill. 1953. *Traders to the Navajo: The Wetherills of Kayenta*. Albuquerque, NM: University of New Mexico Press.

Kelly, Charles. 1940. "Lost Silver of Pish-la-ki." *Desert Magazine* IV (December): 5-8.

Kelly, Charles. 1953. "Chief Hoskininni." *Utah Historical Quarterly* XXI #3(July): 219-226.

McNitt, Frank. 1972. *Navajo Wars: Military Campaigns, Slave Raids, and Reprisals*. Albuquerque, NM: University of New Mexico Press.

Moon, Samuel. 1992. *Tall Sheep: Harry Goulding, Monument Valley Trader*. Norman, OK: University of Oklahoma Press.

Valle, Doris. 1986. *Looking Back Around The Hat: A History of Mexican Hat.* Self-published, Mexican Hat, UT

GEOLOGY

Baars, Donald L. 1983. *The Colorado Plateau: A Geologic History.* Albuquerque, NM: University of New Mexico Press.

_____1989. *Geology of Canyonlands Country.* Lawrence, KS: Canon Publishers Ltd.; Moab, UT: Canyonlands Natural History Association.

Chenowith, William L. and Roger C. Malan. 1973. *Uranium Deposits of Northeastern Arizona.* Grand Junction, CO: U.S. Atomic Energy Commission.

James, H.L., ed. 1973. *Guidebook of Monument Valley and Vicinity, Arizona and Utah.* New Mexico Geological Society, Twenty-fourth Field Conference, October 4-6, 1973.

Witkind, Irving J. and Robert E. Thaden. 1963. *Geology and Uranium-Vanadium Deposits of the Monument Valley Area, Apache and Navajo Counties, Arizona.* United States Geological Survey Bulletin 1103, Washington, D.C.: U.S. Government Printing Office.

BIOLOGY

Anderson, Berniece A. n.d. *Desert Plants of Utah.* Logan, UT: Cooperative Extension Service, Utah State University.

Armstrong, David M. 1982. *Mammals of the Canyon Country: A Handbook of Mammals of Canyonlands National Park and Vicinity.* Moab, UT: Canyonlands Natural History Association.

Behle, William H. 1960. *The Birds of Southeast Utah.* University of Utah Biological Series Vol. XII, No. 1, Salt Lake City, UT.

Mayes, Vernon O. and Barbara Bayless Lacy. 1989. *Nanisé: A Navajo Herbal.* Tsaile, AZ: Navajo Community College Press.

Welsh, Stanley L. 1986. *Flowers of the Canyon Country.* Moab, UT: Canyonlands Natural History Association.

DEDICATION

To Gene Foushee, enthusiastic naturalist, teacher, and premier interpreter of the Monument Valley landscape, and to his patient wife Mary, who supposedly reprimands him with, "Some people don't really want to know that much about rocks"; and

To Susie Yazzie and her family, whose friendship and sharing has enriched the lives of all of us fortunate enough to meet them and whose smiles have transcended language barriers; and

To the emerging tour guides of today, especially the Navajo men and women who are beginning a tradition of sharing their special knowledge with the visiting *Bilagáanas*.

For their help and expertise, thanks to all the great folks at Salina Bookshelf, Inc., Tom Bean, Martin Begaye, William Davis, Wilson Davis, Effie Holiday, Goulding's Lodge, Jim and LuAnn Hook, Kathy Mallien, Alvin Reiner, Randy Scott, the Navajo Nation Parks and Recreation Dept., Deborah Westfall, Bill Williams, Kee Yazzie, Lonnie and Emily Yazzie, and, of course, Ann and Kate.

Library of Congress Control Number: 2004091637

Edited by Jessie E. Ruffenach
Redesign by Kenneth Lockard

Printed in China

First Printing. Second Edition
11 10 09 08 07 06 05 04 10 9 8 7 6 5 4 3 2 1

Published by Salina Bookshelf, Inc.
Flagstaff, Arizona 86001
www.salinabookshelf.com

The paper used in this publication meets the minimum requirements of the American National Standard for Information Sciences – Permanence of Paper for Printed Library Materials, ANSI Z39.48-1984.

ABOUT THE AUTHOR

Growing up as a fan of John Wayne Westerns, Stewart Aitchison thought he "knew" Monument Valley. A little over twenty years ago, through a series of lucky circumstances, Stewart met the extraordinary Gene Foushee, geologist and original owner of Recapture Lodge. Together they have spent many memorable days in the outback of the valley. Through Gene, Stewart now realizes that one lifetime is too short to fully appreciate and understand the remarkable natural wonders and human drama of Monument Valley. But he keeps trying.

Presently, when not writing or photographing, Stewart escorts natural history trips on the Colorado Plateau, Southeast Alaska, and Mexico's Baja. He is author of *Grand Canyon: Window of Time, Death Valley: Splendid Desolation, Red Rock-Sacred Mountain: The Canyons and Peaks from Sedona to Flagstaff, A Guide to Exploring Oak Creek and the Sedona Area,* and *Hiking Arizona* (with Bruce Grubbs), among others. He makes his home in Flagstaff, Arizona, with his wife Ann and daughter Kate.